JABBERWOCKY

JABBERWOCKY

"You have a dreamer's look. You must not dream.
It is only sick people who dream."

—*Salome*, Oscar Wilde.

PRIME BOOKS

TABLE OF. . .

The Harlot's House, *Oscar Wilde*. 7

Summer of Smoke, *Erik Amundsen* 9

Lady of the Lake, *Elise Mattheson* 11

Little Red, *Alison Campbell-Wise* 14

Shapeshifter, *Jessica Paige Wick* 24

Crow, *Catherynne M. Valente* 25

The Forgotten Tastes of Chocolate and Joy

       Jennifer Rachel Baumer 29

Tanguy's Pebble, *Mike Allen*. 39

Confessions of the Man Who Sired a Hedgehog

       Joselle Vanderhooft 42

The Morphology of Snow, *Lynne Jamneck* 47

Kore, *Erik Amundsen* 54

Marching Song, *Jeannelle Ferreira* 56

. . .CONTENTS

On a Day That Has No Name, *Karina Sumner-Smith* . . . 57

Tattoo Destiny, *Maura McHugh* 65

The Waters Where Once We Lay

> *John Benson and Sonya Taaffe* 68

This Reflection of Me, *Catherine L. Hellison* 70

The Woman of Seven Stars Goes Hunting

> *Sara Amis* 74

Revisionist History: A Fairy Tale, *Jennifer Crow* 76

Going Among Mad People, *E. Catherine Tobler* 78

The King of Hell's Daughter, *Shirl Sazynski*. 85

Braggadocio, *Mia Nutick* 89

The Wedding in Hell, *Sonya Taaffe* 91

Under the Influence, *Erzebet YellowBoy* 93

Said the Tree to the Axe(Man), *Nin Harris* 96

THE HARLOT'S HOUSE
OSCAR WILDE

We caught the tread of dancing feet,
We loitered down the moonlit street,
And stopped beneath the harlot's house.
Inside, above the din and fray,
We heard the loud musicians play
The 'Treues Liebes Herz' of Strauss.
Like strange mechanical grotesques,
Making fantastic arabesques,
The shadows raced across the blind.
We watched the ghostly dancers spin
To sound of horn and violin,
Like black leaves wheeling in the wind.
Like wire-pulled automatons,
Slim silhouetted skeletons
Went sidling through the slow quadrille,
Then took each other by the hand,
And danced a stately saraband;
Their laughter echoed thin and shrill.
Sometimes a clockwork puppet pressed
A phantom lover to her breast,
Sometimes they seemed to try to sing.
Sometimes a horrible marionette
Came out, and smoked its cigarette

Upon the steps like a live thing.
Then, turning to my love, I said,
'The dead are dancing with the dead,
The dust is whirling with the dust.'
But she—she heard the violin,
And left my side, and entered in:
Love passed into the house of lust.
Then suddenly the tune went false,
The dancers wearied of the waltz,
The shadows ceased to wheel and whirl.
And down the long and silent street,
The dawn, with silver-sandalled feet,
Crept like a frightened girl.

SUMMER OF SMOKE
ERIK AMUNDSEN

The loud noise jerks your body taut, before
you're aware of the source, and the angels
suddenly in your room, slicing through the bed sheets
punching holes in your wall,
breaking your windows, and the heat follows them in.
Fire is on the tongue of smoke breathing summer, again,
and the nest burns, without its phoenix.

The loud noises wander down the street, leaving holes
and smoke. The angels would dip their wings
in ink to write the words. The angels would dip
their wings in the sea, and I ran,
but the sea was boiling.

Heat is a dog that will run you down.
Fire and smoke become the light of day and dark of night.
Empty streets and clouds of flies and mercy goes, and goes out
of fashion. The manikins melt, like they did
in the old films, the tree drops its leaves.

I learn to fear the day when new garments
will no longer change my appearance. I will disappear,
but nothing I've said can validate. I will dream

of my after life, empty streets, white sky, fire,
clouds of flies

and like the angels, I will learn
to punch holes in the wall, to break windows,
and let the heat come in. I would stand in the street, flames
tickling up between my toes. I have taken poison
to kill my enemies. Now I am the basilisk. Touch me.

LADY OF THE LAKE
ELISE MATTHESON

It was on an afternoon woven of equal parts
Sunlight, aimlessness and proscribed botanicals
Materia medica, ars magicka, efficacious toadstools.
Where the sun came in, I was gilded
Where the shadows fell, he was oak leaf and ivory
A cascade of glossy black down his back
Where the fire inside touched us both, we were molten copper
A burning ship
St. Elmo's fire wreathing the mast, climbing along the rigging
Reflections like flaming coins scattered on frantic waves
Ocean—

No. Not ocean.
I was a lake, I recall—quiet,
Until some idiot threw a sword in me.
There's always some idiot with a sword
Some holy fool, touched by God
("real hard," someone says, and I laugh)
How's a natural phenomenon to have any peace
With people always mucking about making an omen of one
Requiring auguries
Questing after this vision, that revelation

Or simply demanding that one reveal or conceal the artifact of the week?

My sister's a cenote. What's thrown down her, vanishes.
Cold jade waters.
Colder silence within.
I am more temperate, if no warmer.
I prefer the give and take
Though it means my contemplations will be disturbed from time to time
By this one making a deposit
And the other one drawing something forth
A regular lending library, some centuries.

The sword was hot,
Newforged, or so I recall.
There was, as always enough and more to quench the burning brand
To temper the steel.
I think, from time to time, this annoys some of them:
The sheer inexhaustibility
As if it were somehow a reflection on them.
No matter. The sword went in.
As I recall, I gave it away again later.

My old lover the witch in her tower used to tease me
Call me a plaguey thing for giving her gifts away again
Roses cast up on shore, bits of ribbon for the ravens to carry away.

The sword stayed for a while. The hero died.
They do, you know.
It's generally part of the tale, though people may not always
want to hear it.
Swords outlast them as a rule
Lakes outlast swords.

There were currents cold within me
Green weeds wreathed my heart as I took in the sword,
Drew it down
The word "fathom" was not made to describe
What was in my young hero's eyes
They widened as he felt the chill water close over him
I was still too much lake to tell him
That he was a hero,
That heros die.

My silence disturbed him, but the waves we made together
Rocked him to peacefulness
Or exhaustion. No matter.
We came back to ourselves
In a room of dust and oakleaves.
The shadows were longer. We had come very far.
What water was left spilled down my cheeks.
Struck dumb as any oracle, I held him
And with what little kindness I had left
Carefully told him nothing but stories of swords.

LITTLE RED
ALISON CAMPBELL-WISE

The first thing was the fluttering of an eyelid; a butterfly beating its wings against all the darkness in the world. Then, those wings were made into curtains of flesh, thrown wide, letting in moonlight as bright and sharp as a shard of glass, driven into the eye. Then there was the twitching of fingers; the hand, a spider, scrambling against the darkness of unfamiliar ground. Last and first was a breath, a gasp, a scream.

There was no thought yet, only movement. There was a weight in her limbs; they were as clay, bound to the earth. There was remembrance, as well, an explanation of the weight, but there was instinct too, sharp and bright, breaking free the blood beneath the skin, giving her fear of her memories, pleading, with wild cries, that she must keep them locked away. So in the place of thought, she moved, wriggling her toes, like pale worms, breaking up through the dark earth and into the silvery light of the moon.

One arm jerked in spastic, reflexive movement, and dirt rained down upon her so that its taste filled her mouth and its scent filled her nose with the air of rot and death. She rotated a shoulder, arched her back, straining upwards, a creature, breaking free from a chrysalis of earth, being born backwards from the earth into the world.

The rising was slow agony, slow ecstasy, but at last she

stood free, shivering and looking down at the earth from which she had arisen. Her mind screamed its protest against the unnatural thing at her feet, but it could not be denied. The dark place in the earth *had* been her grave.

It was a terrible thing, a shallow thing, unfit for human flesh. For the moment, she was able to look upon it without passion. There was no fear, no pain in the face of memory denied; there was only flesh, shivering in the moonlight. She swayed, toes hanging over the edge of the shallow pit, a wound in the wholeness of the ground. Clothed only in earth of the grave, she looked up at the sky.

Her breath slipped past her bruised lips to wreath the air, giving the illusion of a ribbon of smoke, winding between the stars, which stood as points of infinite blackness, negative light, hung upon the too-white, brightness of the sky. Night in reverse, death in reverse, birth from the grave; she shivered again, memory was fighting to surface in her mind, to show her terrible things she did not want to see. Squinting, she watched the moon behind the running clouds, which cast rings of rainbow light onto the night sky. As she watched, the points of blackness seemed to retreat before her eyes, so that the sky once more became white upon blackness and the moon seemed to move backwards in its course across the sky. She was cold.

She looked down at her toes; they were pale maggots, digging, digging; seeking to retreat back into the earth from which she had risen. The world had begun to spin and there was a sickness rising in her. Memory and thought were returning, refusing, as she had, to lie buried, to stay within. There, upon the mound of earth, which trickled slowly back into the hole in the ground, was a scrap of red.

The red cloak. He had buried her in her own red cloak. He had wrapped it around her bruised and broken body and dropped her in the earth, in a shallow grave that did not even cover her all the way. With her nails, she tore at her skin, as though in shedding her flesh, she could shed the memory and erase the act itself. What good was dying if it did not cleanse you, or set you free? Truth came, a ghostly echo, mocking her silent, questioning cries. She had not died, not really, she had only been born backwards, thrown up from the grave; for even the cold earth did not want her now.

The tears were drying on her cheeks as her eyes searched the ground, looking for anything that might serve as a comfort against the terrible night. Her eyes rested upon the cloak, still half buried in the earth and she reached for it, tugging until it finally came free, showering earth and stones. It was terrible, yes, but it was familiar and safe too and she wrapped it around her thin, moonlit shoulders, and slowly stood. The cloth reeked of the grave, a crimson shroud, but it was all she had against the darkness of the world. He had taken everything else, left her only this, stripping her of name, of body, of soul, leaving only this little bit of red.

She turned, surveying the land around her for the first time. Dark trees reached their arms outward to hold up the sky overhead and in-between their limbs, were scattered stars. One privileged tree was allowed to cradle the moon in its arms, like a newborn child. Looking upon it brought a vague memory of someplace warm and safe to mind, a place among the shadows, a sanctuary of light and love, which called to her now, pulling her out into the night.

Though her body was clumsy and heavy still, she began to move cautiously in among the trees. The memory of the path under her feet was strong in her blood. She had walked this way before, many times in darkness, many times in light. A single way through the trees, salvation and loss, terror and love bound up in one. It was not only the memory of the path that was in her blood, it was the path itself, it *was* her, it was laid for her feet alone and she must walk it, no matter what terror of it was in her heart.

One footfall on the cold, packed ground, one heartbeat, and a word: *Grandmother,* coming sudden and unbidden, without meaning or context to her mind. She stopped once again. The moon had been gliding steadily overhead as she had walked and the forest around her had begun to lose its sense of fear; as though in shedding its darkness literal, it shed its darkness spiritual as well. Into her mind flashed the sudden image of a small cottage nestled in a neat garden behind a sweet little gate with the shape of a heart cut into its center. The smell of things, freshly baked, accompanied the image and the sense of safety, warmth and welcome that came with it was enough to make her break into a sudden run. *Grandmother's house*, that was where she must go, and there, in Grandmother's arms all the foolish terrors of the night would be washed away.

Even in its promise of safety, the path was treacherous, tripping her, so she fell hard, sprawling upon the ground. The breath was driven from her so the world spun in threatening darkness. She was filled with a sudden fear of opening her eyes and turning to see what it was that had made her fall. Like all else though, this too, she could not fight and she turned to see a basket, spattered with mud, empty and lying in the center of the road.

On her hands and knees she turned, crawling, weeping,

towards it, hating and loving it, fearing it and needing it as well. Like the path, it was part of her, like the path, it was darkness and light, love corrupted, turned into hate and fear. Her fingers reached out seeking the rough weave of the basket, crawling over it, like things separate and disconnected from her self, a thousand tiny ants, hungering and searching.

Beside the basket, was a checkered cloth, half buried in the mud, and farther still, a handful of plucked flowers, crushed down into the earth of the path. Catching them in her fingers, she brought them to her lips. Each petal was pale and bruised, grown thin and translucent in the moonlight. She crushed them further; tearing them with her nails and letting them fall even as tears fell, silent, from her wide-open eyes.

"No." She whispered the word. But truth was there, a terrible, hungering thing; a wolf on the path, waiting to catch her in its jaws.

The sky was beginning to lighten now, but instead of receding with the night, the chill somehow seemed to deepen. She opened her eyes, a new weariness upon her now, and dragged herself to a log that lay fallen by the side of the road. The red cloak spread itself around her on the rough seat and she looked down at it, a mixture of regret, sadness and disgust filling her. There was loss woven into the tattered cloth. She fingered its edges, losing herself in the weave of the crimson thread. It had not always been thus though; there was loss, but love as well. Twice, hands that loved her had placed this cloak around her shoulders. And once, love corrupted, had torn it away, leaving her cold and shivering in the dark.

The memories were there, just below the surface, like blood, waiting to break through the skin. It was love that had brought her to this, no, not love itself, but the jealousy it had bred. The love itself had been pure and she remembered it in a rush of images; a strong man, with copper-bronze skin and long dark hair, dressed in the skin of a wolf, with his arms around her, his breath and sweat sweet on her skin. Then there had come the other, the mother, sharp like a knife, shrieking curses and darkness, twisting, tearing asunder all that love. Red was then the color of blood, not love, and the skin of the wolf grew to cover the skin of the man, swallowing the nature of the man as well, leaving only the mindless hunger of the wolf's gaping grin.

She buried her face in the scarlet cloth and breathed deeply of it. The scent of it was no longer her own, nor was it the scent of the one who had first woven its threads to drape upon a girl's shoulders, nor even the scent of her love when he had been a man still and the cloak had been their bed. It was the scent of darkness and death now, of love and light corrupted. Even so, still it defined her, marked her and like the path, it was *of* her and she could not put it aside. She had chosen it and in the choosing, she had chosen her destiny and her curse and she could not turn away from it now. She pulled the terrible material closer around her, binding herself in it like a second skin and lay her head down upon her knees, waiting for dawn.

She must have slept, though she did not remember it, but terrible dreams seemed to hang like a wreath of smoke about her head as she raised it again to the light. Though she could see color blooming upon the horizon, there was still a certain dimness among the trees. She rose and the cloak fell smoothly against her skin. As though she had wept in her sleep and the tears had washed her, her flesh seemed cleansed somehow; made whole and new. The cloak too seemed repaired, as though she had moved backwards in time as she slept. Even in this there was horror, but a subtle horror, for the path, new and fresh, called her ever on, full of unspoken promise and she could do naught but obey. The breeze teased her skin, awakening it, and brought a sweet scent with it, the heady and seductive scent of flowers, flocking to the path's edge, begging to be picked.

She moved distractedly, stooping and catching a flower between her fingertips, twirling it as she brought it to her nose and pressed it against her lips. The scent filled her. There had been flowers before too; flowers that he had brought her, or shown her, flowers she had been lead to? Memory was deceptive false, slipping away, replacing darkness with light; making her mind, like her flesh, new, pure, untouched and naive.

The shadow was still there though, edging the light, confusing the memories, blurring pleasure with pain. She remembered petals falling through her fingers like a silken rain, and then she was falling too. As though it suddenly burned, she dropped the flower from her hand, squeezing closed her eyes once more. She knew what this regression meant, this cleansing of her skin, the fact that her cloak had been made whole. He would be coming for her soon; she had been cleansed, purified, just for him, for the cleansing would only sharpen her pain.

She stood upon the path, her head bowed, waiting as the sun steadily rose. Birds were beginning to fill the air with their song. As though the path beneath her feet were a living thing, an extension of herself, she felt his step upon it, beginning his slow, terrible approach towards her. His casualness infuriated her, building a scream inside of her, which could never be released. He stalked her, as one filled with the certainty of attaining his goal; it was only a matter of time. She listened to his approach, the patter of rainfall, eroding a stone over time and wearing it away.

She could feel his breath upon the breeze and his scent wafted around her, encompassing her. He was all eyes; watching her; all ears; attuned to the beat of her heart, the terror-scream of her soul. The teeth would be next; neither human nor animal now, but a horrid parody of both, unnaturally joined. She shivered and felt the silken touch of flower petals, drawn lightly across the bare skin at the nape of her neck.

Her body stiffened and softened all at once, flowing backwards into him as his touch encompassed her. His breath was hot upon her and full of hunger. Two tears squeezed free, one from each of her eyes, to fall endless upon her cheeks. The points of his teeth touched her skin and two drops of blood sprang forth, one from each, to fall endless upon the skin of her throat.

They mocked themselves now. For the curse, they were mere puppets, silenced against their will and moving in a dumb shadow show, a dark dream of terror that erased love. Soon she would be torn apart, ripped open and laid bare before him, a banquet, spread upon the forest floor. Already the blood was beginning to flow and she was beginning to lose herself, to come apart, to fall away as though she had never been. The sobbing took her, the pain, as always, was terrible and she lived again the pure terror, the torment that had been her fate, since what seemed the beginning of time.

No. It was a faint pulsing thought, a fading star, dying within the blackness of her mind. Once there had been more, once it had been different; she must hold on to this if there was to be any salvation for her. If she was to deny the curse, she must scream against it with the entirety of her body, she must rage and remember, because she was willed to forget. There *was* a time before this, there *was* a before, outside of the eternal now.

But it was so hard to remember. She was forgetting again, coming apart and being scattered like a universe of a thousand shattered stars. A scream ripped free from her throat, filling the entire world and startling the birds from the trees, leaving the forest empty and her, helpless and alone. A scream, a breath, a gasp, a sob.

She was lying on her side now, curled into the fetal position and the cold of the earth was seeping up into her bare skin. It was almost over now. She could feel the life draining away from her, bleeding into the earth. Her body twitched spastically, fighting, despite her own will to let go and have the pain end. It was dark now and the moon was peeking through trees and cloud to peer down upon her, illuminating her body, bruised and broken and dying on the forest floor.

She could feel him moving her, rolling her unresisting body onto the torn remains of her cloak, using it as a sling to move her, dragging it over the rough earth. She opened her eyes, watching the moon, ducking in and out of the trees, like a shadow of herself, running through the sky. She coughed, her lungs contracting painfully and blood bubbled on her lips. There was blood on the rest of her body too, on her throat, on her belly on her thighs, more blood outside it seemed, than in.

She traveled, cradled in a strange nightmare-dream as they moved over the ground. She did not stir as they came to a halt or as she heard him begin to dig, claw-nails, scrabbling in the dark earth, digging a shallow grave. She knew what was coming; soon he would lay her in the shallow earth, where she would die. She would forget and remember and remember and forget and be raised again, moving always back to that place where she would be destroyed, over and over, without end. She might scream and scream, but no one would ever come to save her and nothing would ever change. It would go on like this, as it always had, as it always would, ever after.

She felt the cloak jerked from beneath her and she rolled, unceremonious and unresisting, into the grave, like so much dead, heavy clay. She felt the cloak thrown over her, a thin shroud, hiding her face from the sky. She felt earth scattered lightly on top of her, though it scarcely covered her before he began to move away. Already she was forgotten.

Breath was leaving her. Her back arched once and she fell again into the grave. One arm moved; flung outwards, spastically, reflexively and the cloak was thrown aside and earth showered down on her. She tried to roll away, to move, but already, her flesh was weighted and she was lost to the darkness of the earth around her, cradling her and urging her to sleep. A pale hand, like a spider, scrambled upon a mountain of falling earth. A curtain of flesh fell to cover her eyes, hiding too the silver eye of the moon that hung, silent witness, above her. Breath shuddered out of a body, already gone cold and the last thing was an eyelid fluttering; a butterfly, beating its wings against all the darkness in the world.

SHIFTSHAPER
JESSICA WICK

I'll seal this shape
within my skin: the waves, the wild drum.
I'll leave the ice floes and the rocks:
for fire, foxes; and you
will never know when I shed this shape
and stitched it into shoes.

What isn't shoe, I'll shape instead
into a tambourine.
And when this stifles, oven-hot,
I'll play it play it play it play;
I'll thresh my limbs, and sinews, stretch,
and sing with a hot mouth.

When this seal begins to crack
and you can scrape it thin and clear
and it crumbles like brine beneath your thumb
and you taste like salt
I'll want the waves, the wild drum;
and what, to me, are you?

CROW
CATHERYNNE M. VALENTE

The day I left my husband
he turned into a crow.

His black claws chipped the old
cherry-wood footboard, chest-feathers puffed up
Pluto-purpled, indignant. Came his caws:

How dare you? How dare you?

Ten years I slept
with crow-hands on my waist,
washing crow-eggs in the silver sink,
arranging bits of mirror around the bed
so he could watch himself
while his sooty limbs flapped against me.

Once a month, black feathers
sluiced from me like blood.

How dare you? How dare you?

He worried the bedpost
with a dirty onyx beak.

Yolk-slick eyes accused:
it was mine to keep him a man,
to sit alone at a linen-silent table
and polish my love like wedding silver,
knife by knife. It was mine to keep him whole,
to keep him real,
to nail my fingers to the joints
of a house built for the exultation of crows,
to mind my heart like a tea-kettle,
to listen for its wails and scald,
to pour it out at that empty table,
drop by drop into little black cups
like a dull red leaf.

How dare you fail in these things?

Ten years of bookshelves stuffed
with Poe and Hughes,
nest-twigs clotting the closet-hinges,
feathers in the roof-gutters,
my every dress and sleeve dyed black to match him,
ten years of his screeching to the talon-tallied rafters:

How lovely my voice is!
Tell me, tell me how sweet you find my song!

The day I left my husband,
I drew my knees up against my chest,
covered my head with claw-scarred arms.
I know him so well. I know when to raise up my hands.

His jet-throat worked as he leapt:
pecking at my ears, my elbows,
stamping my shoulders bloody.
His wings beat against my legs,
his cries worked them open—
with the hunger
of a dawn-bird,
he bit into my breasts,
clipped at my lips, scraped scaly toes
against my eyelids.

How dare you? How dare you?

In stories ten years is enough:
enough for penance,
enough for service in a land of foreign officials,
enough for rescue, if there is any innocent left
to be lifted out of the dark.

I ran. He flew behind me, a long dark cry,
bit my shoulders,
clucked pleasure.
I fell on the steep wooden stairs,
fell past black coats hung on hooks, past black hats
and scarves, past black picture frames.
I skidded past black boots and stockings,
black umbrellas barring the door. And out, past the porch,
in the sun—

I knelt on the green lawn,
blood running down my back,

and bent to earth,
black feathers tearing out the edges of my jaw,
spilling from my broken mouth
like guilt.

Behind me, his wings
beat the windows, quills snapping
against four dead walls.

THE FORGOTTEN TASTES
OF CHOCOLATE AND JOY
JENNIFER RACHEL BAUMER

Dancing Jack, wind up boy, edge of town where the harlequins hang. Mask on straight, diamonds over his eyes. Turquoise panes of paint, rhinestones glitter the arch of his brows. Dancing Jack in slicks and sleeks, tights and furs and feathers. He wears satin gloves with rings over and under and chains on his neck and between his nipples and eyeliner around his coal black eyes. He moves like a cat, he flits, he floats, he brings presents to good little girls and boys but there are precious few of those on the Dark Streets.

Dancing Jack, scat like a cat, he blends into the club, all plastic and fluid and the pretty girls and pretty boys and pretty can't quite tells, he brings presents to those and those are plentiful here. Club– slippery, sleek. Stylish and smooth. It's sliver and sleek, gold and green, it's light and dark with drinks that flame and drinks that steam and the pretty girls and boys come here, sleekly ringed, darkly tattooed. Drug patches as jewelry. Flash of silver is a med kit. Flash of chrome is a needle. No diabetics here, no, it's Jack, it's him, and he drops the packages, small squares like candies, fantastic caramels, colorful chocolates, hard candies to suck and the sun comes brighter and the stars shine harder.

She comes to him in his sleep, and always he dreams her

with wings but wings clipped short, pin feathers bruised, molting, damaged. Silver wings that should tower and encase her. She dies a little in every dream and he shudders in half sleeps. In reality she died fast, so fast, she died of turquoise salt water taffy or raspberry shaped hard candy or a trace of chocolate across her tongue. She died because she danced with Jack, a pretty child took candy from his sack, sleek satin gloves tucked treats into her mouth until she choked and cried. And died. And Jack, that moment, harlequin trapped, puppet to their will, victim of his own dreams, trapped in memory, looping through life, no choice but to repeat, to bring his treats to the good little boys and girls and don't knows on the shiny side of town.

Dancing Jack, clickety clack, heels across the sidewalk and Jack in the box, Jack of all trades, Jack be nimble, Jack be quick, Jack turns tricks and hearts and quits. Jack in the box, Jack in *her* box, Jack of Hearts, of Knaves, Jack who saves.

He shoots upward in bed, mouth open in a perfect painted O, scream of negation, denial. Unmaking. He sends her away, sends her flying, he's Jack, in the beanstalk Jack, the one who wins, who runs away and lives to run another day.

The satin sheets are soaked. No denying the dream this time. He sees her again, even with his eyes open. Sees her eyes, wide and blue, and her mouth, pale and hot, the way her lips parted and she accepted the treat, took food from his hand, food of the gods, something sugary sweet and fun to eat only the fun comes after the eating and that time it didn't come at all, that time there was no after, no later, nothing more. He sits in bed, wet satin clings close, and he tries to cry but Dancing

Jack is no longer a real boy and the tears won't come and when he tries to put his hands up to his eyes, to cover his face, to hide disgrace and tears that will not come, the strings on the backs of his hands, the tops of his arms, tangle and knot and the puppetmaster pulls them tight in frustration, irritation. Jack spends the rest of the night awkwardly crumbled at the bottom of the bed where the master flung him in disgust, and the dream comes and goes for him, her eyes, her teeth. The way she died.

She slides inside. No one sees her come in. Bouncers are distracted, too many damn harlequins here, too many masks, to many masked. They have enough trouble without worrying about one lone female slipping past, doorman asleep at the switch or just not paying attention or maybe she's a ghost. Just like her sister.

Looks like one. All whites, night on the town white, stark white, snow white, death white. Long platinum hair, whitened teeth. White fur coat, white satin gloves and tights. White t-shirt, white boots. White knuckles under the black leather gloves where she holds her fists so tight they ache, holds her rage so hard it trembles.

Soon. He should be here soon. She's watched him, followed him, stalked him. Dreamed him. Hated him.

Tonight she'll kill him.

One more time she pulls the photograph out of her pocket, battered thing now, cracked around the edges as if she traveled back in time for the photo. As if she traveled forward in time for this meeting. Juncture. Connivance.

Jack. In the house. In the bar. Jack, adoring audience suspends its bacchanalia.

She follows. Through the crowd. Watches as he dispenses benevolence. This is not Jack as she imagined. A kiss here, a touch there. He cups a cheek, tweaks a nipple. He whispers in ears and they follow him, they'd follow him anywhere. Dancing Jack, treats on the tongue, magic in their mouths.

Touch me.

She shudders. And imagines her sister. And hardens.

Get away from me.

(She never had a sister.)

But he is not coming her way. Too much family resemblance, perhaps. Or something in the way she stares that frights him. He moves herky jerky, trembling limbs and strings a-tangle as if he moves to his own free will.

She thinks it is not her job to punish him. He is not the one she seeks, but the ones who pull the strings.

She will kill him anyway.

Hand on her shoulder and she spins. Him. Came up behind her. Jack in the box. Something evil this way comes. He sways toward her, lovely painted boy. He sways toward her, opens the sack of toys and *Do you want a cookie, little girl?* But he doesn't speak. She wants to touch his arms, the places where the strings or wires poke through, up close they look like wires, the way the skin pulls up and puckers around them. She wants to touch but she'd be tangled and lost, tumbled and bought, and she takes a step back to consider him coldly though her heart pounds and her breath comes quick and her thighs slacken and strain apart. She slicks her lips. She is sleek, is sex, she is this place, white on white, she has nothing to fear. Here. When she looks in his eyes she sees herself. Drowning. Over and over. Lost in the fires of harlequin eyes.

Ducks her head. Listens to her heart pound, listens to it

trip. Clickety clack, the sound of Jack, back. The sound of death and sugar and joy.

He is not a real boy. She can kill him. No one will punish her for disposing of a toy. Her sister, after all, lost to night.

"You knew her." His voice is silk, butterscotch, echoes in her ears and she pulls herself closer. No one comes here if they value life. They come here looking for exit, for escape.

"I know you," he says, and frowns, because they were not just alike. She can see the dream in his eyes, smell it acrid on his skin.

"You don't know me," she says. When she opens her mouth his finger slips in. White satin darkens in her mouth. The glove is satin against her tongue.

The glove is raspberry and apple, chocolate and caramel. She can barely taste the truth under the flavors.

She sucks until there is only cloth, sodden and slick, and pulls back though Jack stands still, his hand held out to her, one finger extended, glove soaked through. He watches, impassive. She turns her gaze off him, but looks back.

"More," she says.

Jack sells dreams. Jack sells lies. All you have to do is look in his eyes. To know. Jack, is back. Under the mask, under the lies. Harlequin diamond mask, painted on. Leather mask, tied on. Tattooed. She wants to reach out and touch it. Turquoise, diamond. It glitters and glows. She reaches out and he takes her hand and she'll let him lead her, take her home. Bag of toys bumps her leg as they walk but that's all right, she's seen his eyes, once he was a real boy and can be again. She'll bring him back, sleepless nights of terror, bring him back and offer him his own Jack.

Midnight streets, slick with lust, shiny black asphalt, turquoise tights, diamond mask, a girl, white on white. Fade into night.

Clickety clack, Dancing Jack, up the stairs, without a care. What waits up there? But she is beside him, her hand in his, and it's like a dream, The dream, like the dream every night with her wide perfect painted pained O of a mouth, fish gasping dying starved for air and her eyes watching him as the room darkens around her and Jack, is back.

You're not her. You can't be her. You're someone who looks like her.

To withhold. No toys, no joy, good little girls and whats and boys. He'll keep his tights on, himself himself. No part of Jack is safe. His hands feed dreams, his legs lead to night-mares, he pumps drugs with his sex. He is a tool, a wire and string thing, a drug himself.

Her lips on his, sugar sweet, the treat he gave her earlier and he strips off the gloves, disgusted, she watches them fall, watches his face, she's so familiar, the feel of her when she sucked his fingers, his satin and silk, so familiar, the way she smells and he'll resist her, he'll send her away.

Wires pull tight. His masters know what he's thinking. They've seen it in his eyes, or the set of his mouth, or read it in the tension of the wires as he fights the configuration and pose. They know. They guess. They mean to trap the girl in white, reel her in, burn her in white flames, it's what they *do* to the slick and alive, the sleek and outside the norm, outside Regular Life, the ones who live and burn and turn from the true, fur and lace, slick and sleek, high heels and chains across insteps and feet, rings on nipples, chains on bellies, chests, threats. Walk away. Run away.

He cannot move. She circles him. He thinks she means to kill him and wants to feel fear. Wants to feel afraid or angry, wants to feel. Anything but empty. Anything but relieved.

She doesn't touch his mouth, painted mouth, candy apple red, dread surges through him, his mouth he could have tolerated.

She doesn't touch his mask or eyes, harlequin eyes. Surprise. She doesn't test for leather or silk or paint or pain. That he could have endured, her hands on his skin.

She touches the wires. Pulls gently. Sensation surges through him. He's hard in an instant. She gently pulls wires that emerge from his forearms, pulls his arms up, arranges him just so, a Dancing Jack, posed and flowed and ready to go. Runs her fingers over the skin where it stretches thin, puckers up around the wires. Runs her tongue after her fingers. Jack gasps. No one plays Jack. He is the consummate player. He sells and teases, taunts and pleases, gives out or holds back, he's Jack, he's the one. Not her. Not this tiny burning girl in white, so like his dream.

She opens her mouth in an O of surprise, locks eyes and holds out one finger coated in cherry juice, in pixy dust, no trust, no belief. Only relief. She slips her finger into his mouth, instantly slick against tongue and teeth, he tastes cherry and joy and chocolate and he looks again at her face and understands, suddenly, hopelessly. She is not here to kill him. She's come to make him a real boy.

The pain surges, every muscle and sinew fights the guidewires. The relief spirals away. Jack bucks like a fish on a line, like a puppet fighting free but he wants anything but that freedom. Anything is better than that. Than the knowledge freedom will give him, the memories free will would release.

The masters fight her. They jerk Jack away, tight wires, Push Her Off, Make Her Go. They want him to pick up the sack, bring Jack back, drug her, tease her, please her, beat her, beaten, bought, discarded, dead. It's what they *do* here on the Dark Streets. His legs jerk out, kick and flail. His arms wrench forward, and fail. To catch her. She's caught him. She holds him, slim, wraith in white, she burns and night around her steps back, picks up his sack, offers him peach and chocolate and hard candy and soft, powdered glitter rock candy off her fingers and all the while the masters fight her. She clings, to him. Not thrown, from him. Locks her legs around his. Her arms around his back. Her face so close to his. The face from the dream. He can no longer pretend. She's not dead. Somehow. Not bought and sold and fucked and led. She's her, she's hers, her own. Not thrown. She holds on tight and whispers in the night.

His name.

"Jack. Come back."

Real boy Jack, on the street. Tired, hungry, no place to sleep. Days and nights dance him, thin, tired, cold but the street has sun, he can tip his head back and see sky, clouds and daylight, lost there, face up towards air, lost in the dream of freedom.

Dark Streets closed to him now, slicks and sleeks and glitter creatures pass him without a word, without a care. No mask, no wires, no bag of tricks. They don't even see him, girls and boys and whats and ifs and lost causes and soon to be's and he can see among them those with wires, those on fire, those whose shoes clickety clack, who carry the sack and run the sweets.

Dark Streets. He waits in the shadows for just a glimpse, girl in white, wild white angel, whoever she is, she took his hand and took his life and Jack walks the streets of freedom with confusion and despair, his eyes turned inward, memory soft, thoughts of lips and touches and sugared joy, of one night of burning and the price of being his own man.

Sometimes he looks across the river and thinks of finding his masters, breaching the Dark Streets. He holds out his arms and searches for pinprick holes, closed now, no wires, no one dances Jack but Jack and sometimes he imagines holding up his arms, *Take me back*. The nights in the clubs, the lonely and the lost and the found and profound and hot greedy tongues and teeth, the way everyone came to him because he was Jack.

He wants that back.

Sometimes. And sometimes he thinks he'll leave the City. Cross the bridge, cross the water, another country altogether, somewhere he's never been. Somewhere he hasn't lost anything yet, or found it, either.

The sound of his footsteps on the street, on the stairs, in the hall. They no longer clickety clack.

But he's still Jack.

Beyond the streetlight he sees a flash of white. Of light. Of burning flame within the night, from one doorway to the next, fleet and swift. It's her. Even from this distance, it's her.

And maybe there's something on the other side. Maybe she'll welcome him back, maybe she'll take him with her when she pulls others across the Dark Streets, into the light.

Maybe she'll welcome him if he comes back.

Real Boy Jack. His footsteps carry him from the streetlight's halo and into the shine and black of the Dark Streets. Toward the clubs. Towards the girls and boys and slicks and sleeks and glitter goths and dark witches and harlequin masks and wires and toys and candy in sacks.

His feet carry him toward the shine and light and noise, and just for a moment, an instant, a breath, his shoes clickety clack.

Jack's back.

TANGUY'S PEBBLE
MIKE ALLEN

They thought de Chirico granted him the gift, and he
allowed everyone to believe, because the truth was far
too strange. He never shared it, not even with Kay,
until too late:

parted from his ship off the Argentine coast,
stolen by the sea gods, delivered, thirsty and freezing,
into the shadow of the Patagonian forest, where a serpent
like coils of fire punctured him in greeting; overhead

the arboreal sea rolled, as he crawled in delirium
over rocky mounds like glowing coral, slipped with a gasp
into sudden grottos, into a world of air like water, of wonders:

beings of plasma and stone; ribbons of curling intellect distilled
from form or purpose; entities of gem-hued mercury flowing
against each other in couplings of love or death; up and down

tossed away like masts in a storm,
         no horizon, unbounded chasm,
warm gold-green stretching beyond sight; he swum, spun,
center of new cosmos, observer of infinities, himself observed—

a small thing, a pebble of liquid, no larger than a lima bean
drifted near, hovered at his fingertips like an inquisitive cat.
Anemone in miniature, his fingers closed—he felt little more
than a soap-bubble burst; fingers splayed again, the pebble gone.

Like lamps extinguished,
    the cosmos dimmed to a roiling blue abyss.
Great hairy worm-things squealed,
    bleeding clouds of octopus ink.
Needle pyramids stabbed the void; wires like marionette strings
grew from nowhere, angled toward him, groped for his limbs.

He fled, in no direction and all,
    steered by fear beyond understanding,
to rouse, thrashing,
    in sheets soaked with ocean brine sweat; daylight
leaned in over the strange adobe arches of Rio Gallegos. Naked,
he stood before the mirror,
    a sea-hardened merchant mariner, Bible

perched by the basin like an accusation;
    stood, watched movement
beneath his skin,
    a throbbing lump the size of a pebble, submerged
into the meat below his wrist. No pain in his flesh, but an ache
that grew, a wanderlust no longer sated by waves against a hull

or foreign ports filled with women of exotic skins. His return
to Paris failed to ease that formless urge, till he read Breton,
felt hope stir. At first his efforts were crude, amateur-Dali,
but his pebbled hand, no matter how he fought, grew more sure,

opening windows to boundless regions he began to see
as home: underwater dreamscapes, crawling crystal cities,
peopled with animalcules of molten stone.
    He married troubled Kay,
herself adrift, who sensed how his soul trawled the deeps,

but couldn't share his mercurial bond, her paintings imperfect
refractions of that subtidal realm. Yet powers there sensed
this congregation of two, warned them of what leered from
over the Alsace; he saw it in the midst of a picnic, black cloud

hovering in the east, grinning, amoebic, exploded cubist skull—
or perhaps a different warning caused his westward flight.
Ensconced in America, he forced his dreams a different way,
exchanging water and crystal for desert and meshing line,

a new space where, perhaps, he hoped to slip away when
the marionette wires latched to him at last; resigned, homesick,
he put up no fight as they dragged him away, leaving poor Kay
to pore in confusion over the quicksilver pebble left behind,

that lodged in her arid dreams like the bullet
in her broken heart.

CONFESSIONS OF THE MAN WHO SIRED A HEDGEHOG
JOSELLE VANDERHOOFT

Like any honest Christian
I wanted an heir
more than I wanted
clear sky for planting,
butter for my seeded bread,
my plump wife's breath
hot upon my knotted neck
as frost crept across the glass
fragile and vine-silent.
Like any honest man
who mops his brow,
looks across the bristled wheat,
and feels his age
I wanted a boy whose feet
would fit inside my insteps,
who could follow me through row and furrow
sewing grain where I plucked up the weeds

God above, I wanted him much more
than I wanted health in my old age,
almost more than my salvation.

Yet, God is a fickle master,
and the saints are cold
as pears that freeze upon the branch.
Though my wheat grew tall
and bristled as a judge's beard
my good wife lay as fallow as the field
where the Traitor swung beneath the crows.

I could grow potatoes in a month,
sweet snapping peas before the old moon's bruises
swelled across his ancient face again.
But children do not crown like cabbages
even when the rain falls thick as flax.
So, I prayed my pater nosters and novenas
until my old knees raveled into ribbons.
When spring ripened in all nurseries but mine
I prayed instead to anyone who'd hear:
let me have a son.
No matter if his face be raw as meat.
No matter if his teeth be sharp as files.
Even if he's pointed like a hedgehog.
Let me have a son.
Heaven did not knock about my ears,
sulfur did not split the steeples.
Instead, the bean seeds burst
and the corn grew beards
as my wife rounded like an onion.

Oh God, how a farmer hopes!
Not for fair weather,
but for yield enough to fill

a mouth, a market place,
his burlap pockets.
Yet when I saw the thing that slid
like water from her ruddy thighs,
I understood why men name the cardinal hope
for a vicious virtue.
I had a son, oh yes,
I had a son.
But not a son enough to pull a plough
or share a stein of beer.
His hands were tadpole-webbed,
his eyes were milk,
and the spine-bones splintered through his back—
very like a hedgehog.

The rains fell soft upon the crops that night.
Only, I did not hear them
nor give thanks.

Oh God, how a farmer hopes
when hail flattens his trellises,
when drought shrivels up his cherries!
How he stamps the spring's weeds with his heel
and resurrect his fences with no necromancy
but the wise use of his hammer and his nails.
Oh, he may brook so many things
but not the one who toddles in his steps,
clawed and bent-backed,
snuffling
for each seed he drops.

I thought,
at first,
That I could tame him
like I do my asses.
If he could not be my son at chapel
my son as I tucked him in his bed
behind the piping stove
perhaps, at least, I could teach him husbandry.
The swine would follow him like dogs,
and the old cock crook his head into his arm
tender as a kitten.
I thought, at least
to do him and a little good.
But of the all the virtues
charity's the second cruelest.

Each time I'd kneel to show
the shooing of a horse, the proper way
to pull the milk from Daisy's udders,
I would see him look at me
not oppressed or cold,
but curious
as if I were an apple out of season.
God judge me though he will, I could not bear it.
God forgive my sins, I could not love him.
I felt it deep as my regret
for ever wishing breath into
the mud-made thing he was.

I think he felt it, too
though I did everything he asked—

buy him bagpipes at the fair,
shoe and saddle dear old Chanticleer—
I think he felt it, too.

Anyway, I did not speak
when he said he would leave me.
I watched him as the sunrise
slanted down the quill-bones of his back
panting him and his retinue of swine
amber, like the still-sleeping earth that housed our carrots.
As he vanished to a point a thought
broke inside me like my former prayers:
how crueler even than charity and hope
is a father's love?

THE MORPHOLOGY OF SNOW
LYNNE JAMNECK

A Curious Creature

I left London, the capital, because of the insidious sense of being swallowed. Everything always crashing and reverberating. Boeings overhead, busses two-wheeling round corners, trains tunneling underground, cars snarling. Like so many metal armored *monstrum*, high on fossil fuels, charging down a kill. Up top they spew noxious gas. Down below they defecate bombs.

I am thirty-one. My body is reactionary. Of late it has made known violent resistance to the junk and the clang of big-city living. Bond Street, Regent Park, Covent Garden; all have lost their sparkle. Too many frequent breakdowns. Too little compensation.

I wake up early in the morning and I want to walk. It's too big here. The concrete's rock-solid. It won't mark the passing of footprints. Everything gets lost in the clamor and the clatter. Sound has mislaid its meaning.

I have never seen clean snow. White, yes.

I'm fortunate enough to be a scientist. We, the curious creature. We study that which others merely observe. We find meaning in ripping the fabrics apart.

Scientists are by no means insensitive . . . Merely driven by an unexplained desire for answers in the abstract.

Nonrepresentational.

Steady Precipitation

"What do you study, Miss Hayward?"

I look at the St. Petersburg children. Their half-formed voices speak as one discordant hive. Their bleached faces are wide with excitement. Big brown eyes like watery marbles. Their English is broken, but I am touched nonetheless. I am a guest at their school. It's an old refurbished factory four blocks from St. Isaac's Cathedral.

"I study snow."

This thrilled them. Their teacher looked confused. A gap in communication; she thought she was getting a *real* scientist.

The children were cheerfully eager for this topic of Western insanity. They gave advice. I might try to find clean snow on the shores of the Baltic Sea. Their faces turned serious eventually. They warned me about the old man with the green beard covered in muck. "The spirit of the Vodyanoy," their Slavic eyes cautioned.

The teacher, obstinate and staunch, discouraged them from believing in such myths.

Slaughter.

Sent From Above

It is not that obscure, is it? After all—it falls from the sky. Just like hail and rain and thunder, and fish and frogs and sometimes birds with broken wings.

Pliny the Elder in the 1st century was both astonished and perplexed at such mysterious phenomena. He called on God and extraterrestrials but neither deigned to send him an answer.

Scientists used words like *troposphere* and *stratosphere* in a game of snakes and ladders with *whirlwinds* and *tornadoes* to calm their suspicions.

Once snow hits the ground it somehow seems less perfect. A sludge here, a slick there. The callous skid marks of sleigh and snowboard. The watery echo of footsteps.

Loss.

Our Lady of Snow

There was a murder. Everyone was very surprised.

I was in Newfoundland at the time. The Middle of the North Atlantic. Where they love the frozen land.

The Avalon Peninsula had been named in honor of Old Avalon in Somersetshire, Glastonbury. Fittingly so. Kings could live here.

This place was Paradise, and to more than just me, for that was the name of town. It wasn't so pretty for the dead girl, alas.

She wasn't a local. No-one knew her. She looked Slavic. I was reminded of the colorless, marble-eyed children and the bearded water spirits.

There were policemen from St. John's. It was very serious. I watched from a bench a few feet away as they examined the girl. Her hair was the color of soot. It bled darkly onto the snow. She looked like a dead princess.

There was a backpack. It lay just out of reach of her stiff fingers. In it they found a pen, an empty notebook and a few scraps of food; an apple. No identification.

There was little blood. It looked like she'd been stabbed. They took her body away. I stared for a long time at the displacement she'd left in the snow.

Tourists were always easy targets. Especially when they

found themselves far from home. I wondered what the girl possibly could have had that had been worth taking. With an abrupt sense of certainty I felt I would never find clean snow ever.

Paradise spoilt.

Euhemerism, Botulism, Dualism

The sallow plastic of the telephone was cold. On the other end, through kilometers of fiber optic cable drifted the disembodied voice of an acquaintance.

"Tony rushed her to the hospital; he was out of his mind. She was throwing up and looking a right mess. He thought she was having a miscarriage. Poor sod; someone should set him right on the facts."

I asked, staring out the hotel window. "When did this happen?"

"Not three nights ago. We was having dinner at the Indian place in Soho. Tony was rambling off to the doctor on duty about Chloe having avoided nicotine and alcohol and god knows what when the buff in the white coat told him to calm down and that his wife had contracted a mean case of food poisoning."

"Thank god. The baby's alright?"

"Baby's fine. Turns out Chlo stuffed herself with a bad tin of smoked mussels the morning before and had a delayed reaction."

"When is she due?"

"Any time now. Hope London's ready for another Crutchley. It's a boy, by the way."

"Good for Tony. Perfect aim." Chloe'd always wanted a boy. Tony's always been a sucker for the name Michelle. Some people think it's wrong but I say God bless Tony Crutchley. He'll starve himself and stick his finger willingly from inside a cage to keep that woman happy.

A silent breath on the wires. "How's Norway? Cold, yeah?"

Sally always reverted to suppressed Pom when she tried to veil the real meaning behind questions. She forgets that I have known both her and Chloe since we were all three tiny monkeys clutching our mothers' paws.

"I'm impervious to cold. There's lots of snow, though."

— *Snow*—

I could practically hear the disappointment and regret in the way she declined to breathe the word.

As we three became older—became women—Chloe has always tried to understand my choices. Sally never proposed to unravel anything she couldn't possibly find her own unique brand of common sense in. I can still remember being appalled when, at the age of ten, Sally had no inkling about fauns and immoral queens and wicked forests that shed their moss and lichen like canopied second skins.

Sally was The Practical One, Chloe was Right Down The Middle With A Single Slap of The Left and I was Long Gone. A right unholy trinity.

To Sally, snow was never anything more than frozen water. Chloe could still imagine that it was something important, simply because to me, it was.

"They pay you a lot, that University, to study ice. Nice job, that."

The vehemence in her voice made my insides hot. "There is a goddamn difference between ice and snow, Sally. A bloody baboon knows that!"

I stared at the phone. I'd yanked it, held it at length, away from my ear as if poisoned. I could hear Sally breathe on the other end. I pulled the wire from the wall.

Disconnect.

So You Think You Know This Story . . .

What tipped people off that I was adopted came down to the hair. Mine was ravensblack. Both my sisters were perfect blondes.

They're both married. One to a barrister who beats her, the youngest to a bruised punk with no money. Guess who's the happier one?

My father remarried when I was twelve. My stepmother doesn't like me. She always said I had too much ambition. Couldn't be good for a woman. She was gloating in a disgusted way when I brought Verity home one Christmas. Said she always knew, and she attributed it to reading. Too many fairy tales. It had led me to wickedness.

I didn't like her either. No big loss.

She was very proud of her real daughters. They were married. Soon they'd both have children.

Twice removed.

Akin To Magic

There is a mountain on the South Pole— I forget its name. Like I've forgotten many things. I've heard people say it doesn't exist. They talk about arctic mirages.

I was there. I found it. And I don't mean the mountain.

The snow there was white and soft as the purest talc. No slicks, no sludge. No blood. No dead girls.

There was a woman, too. She had a name I knew but

couldn't pronounce anymore. She was the personification of my search.

I sat down next to her. "I'm impervious to cold."

The ice moved. The woman smiled.

In the quiet it began to snow. I lay down at the Lady Snærr's feet. The white dragon swallowed me whole and I was complete.

KORE

ERIK AMUNDSEN

"Are you afraid?" I asked,
and she nodded, face of hers gone grease white
fingers trailing, gone numb, blossom dripping.
We were under the ground, then,
in red tunnels without light, so I was protected
from her eyes, but not the rest. No, are you
afraid? Nothing dwells here but the destroyed
and deceased; we saw her with so much to lose
and it offended us. Terrorized. The act of
a moment, a flower pulled, and the trembling,
pink thing, now, rode beside me in this dark chariot.
This smooth pink thing taking up my place,
and a mad-mind yammer "Stop!"
"Turn these wheels around, this must be a mistake."
Tell this thing it is a mistake, but then,
she would still exist and I, where would I be?
I can hardly bear to look. It is not that there are
no beautiful things in my world; those things are
in residence, eternal, dead and proceeded on to zero;
other numbers are too high to count, and count
and count the steps to my chambers the tugs that tear
the cloth on this sobbing, struggling thing,
the number of thrusts, all numbers, all values,

all tumbling to the awkward, staggering zero.
And flight, for there is a remainder, and she does
not vanish, no rendition to nothing for this thing
and I hide, am I afraid? I know not what to do
with the consequence of the difference, the sum
of all steps that led to this place,
and she comes to my table in a black tunic that I
disown as having always been hers, mouth red,
eyes red, and the dark red and pale yellow
of the pomegranate dangling from that hand.

MARCHING SONG
JEANNELLE FERREIRA

And how does the Tsar take his tea?
They came to my mother's apartment, they left
the samovar on the floor hissing,
they carried me by the arms off to the army—
her letters stopped when the city was starving.
And that's how the Tsar takes his tea.

And how does the Tsar take his meat?
They tell us we'll march to Galicia, they say
we'll push on to Prussia, I hope they
still have bread where that is. Last night
the stew and our boots filled with maggots.
And that's how the Tsar takes his meat.

And how does the Tsar sleep at night?
Dogs howl when we come marching, howl through snow
out at nothing. We can wait. We will always be marching.
They say his pearl-pale smiling son is ill,
they say God save him.
And that's how the Tsar sleeps at night.

ON A DAY THAT HAS NO NAME
KARINA SUMNER-SMITH

In the morning of a day that has no name, no number, I cast my nets far into the bay. Hand-woven things, a mess of rope and scrap, they float for a moment like scum before sinking, trailing small bubbles as they go.

I should not wade so deep, the voice of my fearful body cautions me. I stand in water up to my chin; the ground beneath my feet is soft and mucky, oozing between my toes. To throw the nets I had to raise my hands high, my tossing motion an awkward flailing of arms. I was not born to such labor, these hands trained to wonders that have nothing to do with fish.

To fix the nets, spread them so that food and other more important treasures are caught in the tide, I have to wade deeper. Be careful, the voice whispers. Not so far.

Of what should I caution myself next? Do not fish deep waters without a boat. Do not swim alone.

Perhaps if I fish long enough, deep enough, I will find a boat. Perhaps I'll find a friend, or his bones.

I go out every morning and evening with my nets and my line. I sometimes catch fish, but it is rarely fish that I am looking for.

I have watched the waters carefully. I've climbed to the top of the tallest tree, its bare, storm-broken limbs scratching my arms until I bled, and searched the waters for any sign of shadow. I have watched for sharks, for whales, for porpoises—anything, driven by hunger and desperation, that could pose a threat. Anything, driven by need or fear or loneliness, still alive. I have seen nothing.

My only companions in the tiny bay are fish. They are skinny and wasted, like me; they taste of ash and mud. Their numbers were always few, but now they are becoming skinnier, weaker; their nibbled bones squish and bend beneath my fingers.

When I eat, I eat in silence, alone.

After spreading the nets and wading a short distance away, I cast my line: a long, knotted string made from bits of twine and grass and hair. It is not strong, but strong enough; as the sun rises high above the horizon, there is a tug and hand-over-hand I haul my catch aloft.

I watch the fish at the end of my line. Its mouth, impaled with a hook made from a twist of sharpened metal, gulps at air. Its gills move wetly, flapping open and closed against scales the color of damp stone, but its silver eyes stay perfectly still. Can a fish see in air? I wonder as I watch it. Can it see me seeing it?

It twitches its tail once, twice, three times, and then hangs there spinning, gills opening and closing, as if this lethargic struggle is all it can manage.

In the wake of the end, the first word to lose its meaning was mercy. Or perhaps it was cruelty. Staring out across the water at the sun, the fish hanging limp from my line, I cannot remember the difference. They are the same stamped, tarnished face on a coin, staring blindly outwards.

I look at the fish, I look at the sun, and time goes by. The fish hangs still on the end of the line for many minutes, its movements long since ceased and my feet wrinkled by their extended submersion before I at last declare it dead and begin to wade ashore.

I have difficulty recognizing death, these days. This is not comforting, nor distressing; it is merely a fact.

Here is another: the fish are poisoned.

Everything is poisoned, in one degree or another, but of those things that remain the fish are the worst, swimming and eating and breathing in that massive churning body of disaster and decay that I still—clinging to my roots and abandoned past—continue to call an ocean.

And yet I am hungry. I must eat. My stomach cramps in hunger, terrible and twisting, and what is there to eat but dying fish, poisoned fish?

There is little left. That which is green turns yellower by the day, leaves crumbling at the edges, algae turning brown and haunting the water in clouds. The fish eat the bodies of all things larger than them, all the great and fast things that were granted a death that can be called "quick" in comparison to this. There are plenty of corpses in the ocean.

Plenty of dead fish in the sea.

It is only right that I eat them, that I dine on poison and drink deep of death. For I long to reach the ending, and the poison that kills is mine.

The evening nets bring me treasures: a belt buckle, a cracked perfume vial, the leather sole of a single shoe. And a ring.

It is caught in a clump of rotting seaweed, so buried beneath

59

the slimy strands that it's only the slight glint of gold that keeps me from throwing the tiny thing away. It takes many long minutes to free the ring from the tangle, and then I hold it aloft, peering at it in the silence. Once it held a stone but now the upraised metal claws are empty, only a last strand of seaweed caught in their grasp.

A wedding ring, I think, though in truth this small band of gold could have had many meanings, many possible owners. Yet it is a wedding I see, the image hovering before my eyes like an illusion, and I can almost hear the soft words of spoken vows, promises of love. I close my eyes and curl my fingers around it.

Promises are things that cannot be kept, cannot be held. They rot, just as flesh does, and as strangely; and the metal that we dare call symbols, they are more transient than cloud. There is more sense in an unopened bottle, a child's carved toy, a half-burned candle caught in nets of rope and sand.

I realize I am shaking.

And in a moment that I don't know whether to name fear or guilt or something else entirely, I throw it back. The ring lands in the deeper waters of the bay with barely a splash, and vanishes.

I've made promises. Too many, perhaps, and destined to be broken.

Once I promised to guard my city, giving my life and gift to those faraway towers of soft gray stone. Once I promised to do no harm, and once I promised to heal the sick and ease the dying, and once I promised to make my one terrible mistake right again, no matter the cost. I promised to make this right.

I strive to regain my seeming immunity, for numbness and

the ability to feel no pain, as the dying ocean mocks me with its gifts. I've made many, many promises and I feel them all crumble in my mouth as I wade slowly ashore, the water-logged nets trailing behind me.

Yes, this poison is mine. I found it, and I let it free.

It does not matter that it was to be a preventative, a cure. It does not matter that people were ailing, suffering, beginning to die from a winter sickness that had no ease but raced across the countryside like fire through dry tinder. And I, with my talent and my kindness and the ego I thought benevolence, I had promised to keep them safe.

No, these things do not, cannot matter, for when my cure seemed to be working and I and all others like me were too slow to catch the disease's far edge, I made a choice. A decision. Without knowing the consequences, without asking permission, I put it into the water supply.

Exile. Had any of us known the full extent of the coming ruin, surely they would have killed me, and I should have thanked them for such a gift.

Though I saw the people of my beautiful city begin to sicken and die anew, I was not there to see this new disaster spread. I did not see the ancient trees begin to wither, their leaves to curl and crisp. Lost and exiled in this distant place, I was no witness to the slow death of the fields, of the crops and forests and the very earth in which they grew, nor the slow death from hunger and the poison that spread from the place I once called home.

No, I was not there, but I consider my absence no mercy. When I close my eyes I can see the land I left behind. I have heard the screams, the groans and the cries of the dying; I have lived the destruction over and over again in sleep. Magic dreams at first, and then merely strong dreams, telling dreams. And dreams need not be real to be true.

The magic is dead now, too, poisoned as surely as the people and the ocean and the trees. I feel its ashes deep within my bones and my belly; where once there was fire, now there is only something cold and hard and gray.

If I could, I would dash my head against the sharp rocks of the bay, or find a sliver of shale with which to open the thin flesh of my wrists. If I could I would hurry the inevitable conclusion, follow everyone and everything I have known and let the poison spread without me, let the death go on in my absence.

But there is that promise, those dry and bitter words I spoke to people who had already turned away. It is too late now to save anyone, even myself, of that I feel sure; and yet there is always the chance that the morning tide could bring me a solution: a stone, a relic, a body, a note. Some idea, some inspiration, something I have not tried.

I eat my thin fish in silence, and envy them their ends.

On a day that has no name, no number, for I have made all such distinctions irrelevant, I cast my nets far into the bay and catch a fabric ruin that was once a robe. An enchanter's robe, a wizard's robe: a silken swirl of white and gold and blue.

I once wore cloth such as this, and crowds stepped back to let me pass.

It is ripped and torn, the robe's fine beadwork embroidery gone for but a few seed pearls whose silken knots refuse to be torn free. I hold the wet fabric to my nose as if it might still hold the smells of civilized life, the spicy scents of magic and incense. It is cold and heavy, dripping, smelling only of the ocean's decay, and yet I draw it around my bare shoulders and raise my arms to the sky as if magic could still rise from me, as if an antidote might lift from my withered skin like steam from a hot stone.

I am a child in a costume, a clown whose antics draw no laughter. Mine are the only eyes to see and if I could, I too would turn away.

When I have no energy left, I sleep on the sand. I dream. I stare at the horizon and wish and hope that the heat shimmers I see in the distance are truly sails. Let them be pirates, let them be mercenaries, let them be vigilantes come at last to carve justice from my ailing flesh. I would welcome them all with open arms, even as they killed me, just to see a person's face. Just to see someone living, breathing.

I write my confessions in the sand and each day the waves wash the words away.

There are none left of whom I may beg forgiveness.

On a day that has no name, no number, I wake and cannot stand. There is pain in my belly far worse than crippling pangs of hunger, and pain in my arms, pain in my legs. I try to struggle to my feet, and thrash helplessly in the sand.

I hear a moaning, a terrible sound like an animal in pain. There is no sense in the groans, no words, no sign of intelligent life —

It is, of course, me.

My brain thinks slow and gray thoughts as my mouth works, shrieking and dribbling, without me. My legs convulse, feet digging furrows, then spreading wide to sweep the sand into a shape like a snow angel's dress. I smell my own sour sweat, the dark stains on my clothes, the wetness of my skin. My chest heaves with strange breath, the convulsing of my diaphragm.

This body has slipped away, to piss and vomit and drool into nothingness. Only my eyes and brain are sane now: right eye, left eye, and mind all staring upward. Repentance in small movements. In clarity. In stillness.

The sky is clouding over.

I wonder if it will rain.

TATTOO DESTINY
MAURA MCHUGH

In modern Ireland
The Morrigan runs a tattoo joint
Where she inks and pierces
Affluent young flesh,
And grins as she digs the needle in.

Her incisors are capped
With cursive silver spirals.
"Wicked", her clients groan,
When her lip curls back
As she draws blood.

She never speaks.
Merely nods at the designs,
Or ignores them completely,
To puncture skin
As she desires.

Those who recline
In the worn leather chair
Swear the swirling scenes
Carved on her muscled arms
Flow like film as she works:

Storm-borne ravens hover
Over fields of carnage
Where armies, champions, lovers,
Collide
In eternal war;

A dark woman
In a flapping feathered cloak
Oversees ruin and triumph
In splendour
From her high fort.

At night she haunts clubs,
Sits in a shadowed corner
Whiskey in hand
And watches her potentials
Gyrate and churn.

She does not consort
With bright young mortals.
They would extinguish—
Ecstatic—
With a kiss.

They are canvases
For her Art.
Across their contours
She maps lines of fortune,
And vortices of fate.

Her skin spells
And pierced patterns
Invoke a future
Where she reigns anew:
Mighty; dreadful; revered.

Until then she pays rent,
Taxes and utilities,
And recalls Empire,
As she inscribes her destiny
In blood.

THE WATERS WHERE ONCE WE LAY
JOHN BENSON AND SONYA TAAFFE

memory of salt and sea
taste first insistent
then familiar delicate
undertones of green
quiet waters
where once we lay

Light through language
clarifies mother-of-pearl
and sepia, remembrance
cradled like the moon
in the arms of the tide:
so too us, where now
the waves boom empty
at my feet.

half-void of indecision past
first breath bubbled through brine
choked throat, tide receding
warm lassitude of waves left behind
I kneel to write letters in the sand
with kelp torn from my eyes

The sea urchin's skeleton
I picked, broken-spined,
like a discarded offering
from the fine slurry where
darkening waves pull back:
a cold drip of salt between
my fingers, no messages
from this bare strand,
barren sea.

organs, tissues
lonely dissolution
daddy, tell me bones
now bones alone remain—
and memory till
tide takes both away

Wind over my face, salted
chill as tears; driftwood
rolling where my footsteps
filled with seeping tide.
The night sea gives
nothing back, not even
comfort. A razor clam
shell. Pebbles.

kelp-litter in the sand.

THIS REFLECTION OF ME
CATHERINE L. HELLISEN

I live in a bone house.

The last room—that's mine. You can tell because the brass handle is still shiny, polished by my master's palms. At night I walk down passageways tarry with decay, with the years' grime. I pass the other doors. Their silent wooden faces.

All rooms in my house are quiet.

The master is away in his black-rigged ship, held aloft with hands grey and green in the dawn. In my mind, I see the waves' fingers turn white as they clutch at the decks, perhaps pulling a man overboard.

I close the dream, and step out into the hallway. The floor is old, the boards worn thin at the edges, not meeting. If you drop something small, it will be lost to the people that live beneath.

The others up here are all dead. Seven girls brought to me, their dowries gather dust next to their bones.

Sometimes, I go to look upon them, to glean what I can from their faces, from the way their screams have solidified in the dusty flesh. The door to their burial room is never locked, for he knows how I like to sit in their silence. I'm happiest when it is quiet, when I can lean into them, nestled close, and hear only the muted call of nightjars or owls. I curl up to my favourite, lean into the length of her body, and pull her arms

70

carefully around me. Ivory clacks, and dust falls. I must move with painstaking sloth, for fear I break this delicate embrace. Ah, love is such a brittle thing.

Outside, far below me, the streets are quiet. No-one walks along the cobbles. Only the wind comes salt-laden to the window, and whispers in my ears. I nod, and leave my plaything, my sweet girl, to go and see out the narrow window. Grime has shuttered the glass, and it takes all my thin-armed strength to push the window free. I lean over the ledge, gazing down to the distant water.

Moonlight silvers the city, edging her spires and turrets with halos. The sea speaks again, the wind carrying her message to me. And there! I see the sails in the harbour, silhouettes against the streaked horizon.

The master is home.

"She's a pretty one," he says. He knows I saw him bring her in. I always watch.

I see her only briefly, shining under her cloud of dark hair. The others were so pale, so gentle, I could not help but be drawn to their cleanness; the soft golden edges of them. I do not answer him, instead I look in the mirror, and comb out my hair with the new ivory-handled brush he has brought me. I like this gift better than the other. Under the moonlight, my hair shines with a black so rich that it seems almost blue.

The girl is an intrusion. She breaks the quiet with her childish noise, flittering as she does from room to room, like a black dove trapped in a locked house. All thundering heart beat and the clatterclap of wings.

At night, when he should be with me, my master ruts in her bed, his pale arse like flyblown fruit between the dusk of her thighs. I stop watching through the rotted boards. The ivory handle breaks when I fling my brush across the room and into the scowling face I see reflected at me from the unmarked mirror. The swarthy face glares back and then she is gone. I press my ear to the boards.

"What sound was that?" Her voice is high and cool.

"Ah, nothing, nothing, my sweet. A bat maybe, or the baker's cat running from roof to roof."

"If there are rats in the attic, my love, I'll instruct the servants to set traps."

"Not rats, my sweet. I told you it was but the baker's cat. We'll hear no more sounds, see?"

I listen from the walls, from the cracks. The dove coos, trying to keep him to her bed.

"Must you go?"

"If you like the finery I bring you, then I must," he says. "No seas give up their treasures without a fight."

"You said you were a merchant."

"And so I am."

My black prince merchant, with his ship of darkness, has set sail once more. He's left her alone in the house, the servants instructed to obey her.

The first night he is gone, I see her rummaging through my master's things, her fingers quick as darting fish. She reminds me of a dove no longer – the frantic wings have given way to furtive glances. She is a ship's rat, scratching through treasure.

"Do you have the key for the attic?"

The servant shakes her head, mute with fear. All these are loyal to me, they will not speak to her.

She has found it while I sleep. My master's key.

I hear the tread of her slippered feet on the stairs that lead to my house of bones, and I am instantly awake, curled and ready as a cat.

The key slides into the oiled lock; just the faintest snick of sound, the barest tumble of gears, and the door is opened. She carries a candle, or perhaps an oil lamp. The light spreads disease into my muffled gloom, infecting with its flicker.

The shadows pull around me, cloaking me with their soft quick fingers, and I pad after her as she makes her way with halting steps down the passage of my home.

Tonight her arms are too stiff for love. I lay the girl down, ease off the embroidered slippers my master gave her, unbutton her chemise. I stretch out against her, pressing my chest against the soft swell of her, against the ripeness of her body, before I pull a silken blanket over us and fall asleep with my breath fluttering her lashes.

Light comes stealing into my house. Even the morning bird-song can not break my mood. Looking down at the girl's face, so peaceful in repose, I can see now the beauty that my master saw. She is prettier than all the others, this reflection of me.

THE WOMAN OF SEVEN STARS
GOES HUNTING
SARA AMIS

Do you regret turning your ear to the dark,
you who were born the morning star?
Do you regret it, peacock woman?
Did you forget yourself in your descent?
Did the gold rub off your skin?
Did you consume your warrior's heart?

Queen of heaven they called you, the woman of largest heart
Your heavy scented hair grows dark
and curling like vines across your skin
We look up at the falling star
Burning even in descent
And say yes, that is a woman.

All lights may be extinguished, even yours, star woman.
You surrounded emptiness with your heart,
and listening, began your descent
to the no return, the dusty dark.
You came down like a visiting star
Like a royal barge, a queen, perfume on your skin

I know you felt it on your naked skin
The disdain of that envious woman
For you, the morning and evening star.
Your pride, your arrogance, your willful heart
Like hers, the woman whose home is the dark
This is where you come to in your descent

You struggled to rise, in rage from your descent,
attacked her, and she removed your skin
Hung your corpse above her gate in the deep dark
All lights go out here, even yours, sky woman
This is what happens when your heart
eats dust and emptiness. You forget you were ever a star.

Two companions come to guide you—only flies, not a star;
Small and wily enough to follow your descent
without notice, wise enough to weep and turn the heart
of your dust gathering sister and beg from her your skin.
Let the water of life turn you back into a woman.
Let your woman's feet bring you up from the dark.

A heart can be shaped and burning like a star,
It can open up the dark and plunge into descent
As I am a woman, this is my return, my holy skin.

REVISIONIST HISTORY: A FAIRY TALE
JENNIFER CROW

Once, the mirror opened on new vistas:
blush-red and snow-pale, all the autumns
and springs of the world. I showed her
the future, cities on the moon
and men in flight, a library in the hand
and a promise on the lips
of heaven. She laughed
but not for joy, teeth flashing in my shadow,
for she had already followed
my woodsman into the green fastness
of the forest, and carried the scent
of crushed flowers on her skirts.
Only her own future held her gaze,
with its ball gowns and pretty mares, silks
and armor-clad princes—and when I
showed her
warned her
of the sweet-salt scent of sex
the damp tangle of sheets
the pain of childbed
the gush of fear between the legs
the nights awake, lying still
lying

regretting—
all that, and she laughed.
And when the prince choked her
for an apple, for a simple token
of unrequited love,
the mirror reflected her fear
back to her in a thousand facets,
and she sent blame to my door
like the boxed heart of a deer
caught running among the trees.

GOING AMONG MAD PEOPLE
E. CATHERINE TOBLER

At night, Alice liked to climb up into the chimney; the cater-pillar agreed to meet her there. Crouched on a jutting brick, she took her tea, and he took his pipe. The very nature of the chimney made the pipe bearable; were they in her parlor, Alice would have forbidden it. It had a terrible smell and left her lightheaded.

Caryl, the son who hadn't died in the Great War, knew nothing of these meetings in the chimney. If he did, how he would have wailed. His continual fretting was bad enough, but to learn that his mother had taken to furtive meetings with a caterpillar in her chimney would have been his undoing. She didn't like to imagine his teeth cutting into his bottom lip or his hands opening and closing on thin air as he sought a comforting answer.

"Mother, please, we should really tidy you up before Emma comes."

She shooed his hands away. They were clammy today. Caryl grunted, standing back with clammy hands on flat hips, and she grinned.

"Don't grunt," was all she said and settled herself more deeply into her chair. She glanced at the clock, but it revealed nothing new. The sun was up, her next meeting with the cater-pillar hours away. She closed her eyes.

Caryl couldn't leave well enough alone. He saw no need for her to nap the day away, especially when he was permitting Emma to visit. Emma wasn't often allowed inside and Alice thought this a pity, for she had many stories to share with the child.

Alice wanted to take her on summer rowboat rides and find a pool of shade in which to say "once upon a time." Caryl believed such things foolish, occupying hours that could be better spent organizing one's socks.

"Leave me to sleep and dream, won't you?" she asked as Caryl continued to fuss. He was attempting to wrench her feet from her ankles. Alice kicked at his hands, a very unmotherly thing, but she preferred her feet precisely where they were.

"How long since you've bathed? Is this soot?" He grasped the hem of her skirt and she kicked at him again.

"Nothing you need concern yourself with. Nothing."

Her gaze darted to the end of the settee, watching a smile slide behind and then under, the whisper of an unseen tail disturbing the dust. Alice tensed. She still didn't know if she trusted that cat.

"Please, your shoes," Caryl said quietly, but Alice wouldn't quit kicking her feet. He finally abandoned the shoes to look around the parlor and its disarray. "What have you done in here?"

"Nothing."

"Indeed—"

"I remember a teacup," she said, eyes wandering in concert with Caryl's. "I cannot find it. It was nothing fancy. These are all too bright." She gestured with one hand and sent a stack of teacups crashing to the floor. Porcelain flecked everywhere, like sharp snow.

She didn't have a matching set of anything, be it teacups or silverware. Alice didn't know how she had obtained a single piece of everything she possessed. When she thought backward it was not porcelain she sought, but a gently moving boat, or the younger Caryl who never left her side and seemed interested in every word she had to say.

"Emma will be here soon," Caryl reminded her, "and you've missed her, haven't you? She won't want to see you sooty and torn."

"Fuss all you like but I shan't budge until my teacup is found."

The stacks of teacups within the room could not be counted, unless one had countless days in which to count. Caryl looked around the room and Alice wondered if he found it as endless as she did. Filled to the brim with teacups and no two alike.

Alice fingered the shards of broken porcelain. Caryl snatched her hand back from the ruin.

"Indeed," she said, "if I cut my finger too deeply, it will bleed." She tucked her hand into her skirt.

Perhaps today was not the best day to bring Emma, Alice thought. The parlor was a mess, her clothes were sooty, and surely the sun would sink soon. She had a meeting to keep and a teacup to find.

"Can you tell me what your teacup looked like?"

She laughed at this, for if she could tell Caryl what it looked like, then she could find it on her own.

"Don't grunt!" He was always grunting like a little pig. She patted his cheek, warmer than his hands, and clicked her tongue.

"We shall start at the beginning," she said, "and work our

way to the end." Alice only knew the sooner they began, the sooner they would finish. That was logic.

"There are two very special young men coming this evening," she said as Caryl took up a stack of teacups.

"Who is coming? Do I know them?" Caryl's forehead creased with a frown.

"You know them quite well," she said, but did not elaborate, for surely he would know of whom she spoke. She looked instead beneath the settee, to see the gleam of a smile between Caryl's ankles. Once upon a time she had taken comfort in seeing that cat, but now its smile chilled her.

Oblivious to the cat, Caryl offered the first teacup in his stack, a brassy mermaid swimming in a topaz sea.

"No!" She slapped the cup away. It shattered on the floor, scattering more porcelain snow into the air. The cat's smile faded just a little.

"If you mean to continue on like that, we'll stop right now," Caryl said. He lifted the next cup.

Alice forced herself to look at the cup and not the cat. "It was not white, and did not have blue flowers. It is like a dream, this cup. I can almost picture it, and then it slips away. Roots and crumbling dirt."

As soon as she said it, she wished she hadn't. She scrubbed her fingers across her scalp, expecting to dislodge dirt and roots. It was only fine silver strands that twined her fingers when she finished.

Caryl said nothing; she didn't expect him to. He didn't like to talk about her youth. There was a time he had enjoyed her stories, but he now required glasses to see, rather than his imagination. Close your eyes, she wanted to tell him, and look, but he wouldn't.

"It is none of those cups," she said. "I feel that we may look forever and will not find it. Perhaps I left it somewhere else."

"Then indeed we may look here forever and not find it, and you will still not be ready for Emma when she arrives. And you wonder why she does not come."

"I understand perfectly well, you do not bring her. There is so much I should tell her."

"That is why I do not bring her. She doesn't need to hear your stories, Mother."

Alice's hands fisted into her torn skirt. "Think how wonderful she might find them. I know you don't—"

She looked at her son, and wanted to tell him about meadows and storms and doors too small to fit through. But he would turn away, speaking of ledgers from work, of other commitments, of Emma and his wife and how he had to rush to them. Alice too wanted to rush, but pressed herself deeper into her chair.

"I know you don't," she whispered and said nothing more on the matter. She thought instead of the caterpillar and his round-about talk and how she needed that right now, but could not have it, for the sun was still slanting through her one parlor window.

She curled a hand below the chair's cushion, and her fingers came upon the hard round edge of a small teacup. She started, but did not move as Caryl held another cup up for inspection, this with bright orange polka dots.

"No," she said. "That's not it." She rather hoped Caryl would stay all afternoon looking through the cups. Even if he didn't allow Emma to come, she would have Caryl, a blessing if clammy in his kiss.

Caryl worked through the entire stack of cups on his lap

and when Alice had denied each one, he carried the stack into the kitchen. When he returned, he took up another stack.

Alice denied every cup, for though each was familiar, each was also not the cup she remembered. That cup, small and plain, was buried beneath her cushion, home at present to her fingertips and a collection of gray oyster shells.

Alice did not touch the shells, though she knew them to be there; they would make a terrible noise, one that frightened the caterpillar, and she could not have that.

"When do you think Emma will arrive?" she asked and looked out the window, where she spied a strange man in her garden. "Who is that man?"

Caryl glanced out the window as he lifted another stack of cups. "Your gardener."

"No, I have no gardener, I like it wild, you know this." The words came out with a strength that surprised both of them. "He has crushed the pansies and oh—the roses…"

"Wild is one thing, a jungle is another. He's taking fine care."

But the caterpillar liked the pansies, said their purple faces made his green all the more bright.

Alice touched the oyster shells now, carefully taking one into her palm. She squeezed until its rough shell cut into her skin. She had eaten every one.

"Why must you?" she asked. "My garden was fine."

"Mother, is this your cup?"

"Yes," she said and said nothing more, didn't even look at the cup. She wanted this vile person gone, she wanted to be left to her shells and her flowers. It took all her strength not to fling the shells at his horrible pinched face.

Caryl kissed her cheek. He dropped the teacup into her lap

and left the room. Sometime later, Alice heard the closing of a door. Alice knew that Emma had not come, and would not. There would be no stories that afternoon, nor any other, she supposed.

She sat in her chair and waited, listening to each passing tick of the clock, taking them for her own heartbeat as she watched the fading of the sun through her parlor window. She watched the cat's smile beneath the settee; where once he was filled with advice, the cat now sat silent.

When at last the room was dark, she withdrew her hand from the cushion. She kept the oyster shell with her, for perhaps the caterpillar would like to hear that story. It had such a sad ending, but then most things did, Alice supposed.

Alice stood from her chair and the cup fell from her lap, breaking to unnoticed, countless, pointless pieces at her feet. She crushed them on her way to the chimney.

It was never a tight fit and only at the flue did her breath catch a little. She pushed past the slight narrowing, climbing into the cool darkness, up to her brick where she sat, and quietly awaited the caterpillar.

THE KING OF HELL'S DAUGHTER
SHIRL SAZYNSKI

To write a poem about him would be an obscenity,
she thinks
but still she does it in her way
less often, now, of late

Her small, sharp-angled feet tread down
the flagstones of a forgotten corridor, then stair
a winding snake which does not sink to unplunged depths but
highest
closest to his home

Sometimes there is a weak current where the air blows fresh
and cool instead
when the tang of fire blossoms can be forgot
for a faint, foreign whiff of grass, good loam
and narcissus in the spring
    —this, her only mercy
 is no mercy
 and done for old times' sake

the unseen door obeys her lips and gesture
this piece of untaught sortilege
her kind were born to know

No light comes to this cell
ever
save from where his wings once were, a diffuse glow;
it does not matter. He lost that sense long ago.
but still she dims the lamp, lays it down with a small scrape
along with the implements of his freedom—
blindfold woven from the very hair of night
from the hydra's fangs, her needles
a box of pinions he should recognize
barred bright as a hawk—(she keeps them to forget)
though he longer has tongue to confess
his greatest crime of all
the shackles, caked with rust might crumble
at a struggle (should he remember how)
or made of less
than the craftiest deception,
of a weaker stuff
than hate
gently she fingers the ruin of his back
rewarded by a shudder of recognition
though he does not lift his head, nor lean into her touch
as once he might

the hair, like summer, has grown long again since her last visit;
it must sting where it falls
she brushes it aside to seek a loose, bleached splinter
jutting low between his shoulder-blades
remembering its scent
a taste of heights and colors she must never seek
soft as zephyrs against her tawny breast.

and the wings which sheltered her in secret
bore her up to see
the glory of the stars at night.
Hidden in a blank of cloud they danced and listened
to the song, ten-thousand miles past her kingdom
(this heaven's last joke).

A small gasp as she plucks it, the only sound he'll make—

And she considers
freedom—

the hollows of his ribs before her, the knotted column of his
throat—
a single stroke—

but, no.

She draws the splinter 'cross her hand then lays that hands
upon his cheek
one side of his face a travesty, the other half preserved
though the blue of his eye has since diminished
from a winter's midnight

she solemnly brings that hand to his dry lips and bids him
drink
her firey blood and see once more
her silhouette
the wonder of caverns deep
of silent pools, lush gardens of chrysolite and jade
—at this he always weeps—

and at this, her expression will not change
kissing, now, the ruined half of his lips
his tears she gathers in a vial
(she never tells him this)
one day to pour into the King of Heaven's wine
mixed in with her own

BRAGGADOCIO
MIA NUTICK

A glass coffin? Bah.
How the tales grow over the years.
As I recall it was a pallet,
poles and an old blanket.

It's true that I was hunting
when I found her in the forest
carried by a group of stunted little men . . .
inbred hillfolk.

My men dispatched them
while I attended to the girl.

It's true she was a rare beauty . . .
is still, of course, don't you agree?
All that black hair, that pale skin . . .
of course then she was just a slip of a thing
dressed in rags, and none too clean, either.

And her condition . . . warm as a sunny day
but still as death.

You'll never know, boys,
you'll never know the relief . . .
no tiresome wooing,
no silly tears, no contrived struggle
or protestations of virtue.

It was no chaste kiss that woke her, boys,
but the vigor of my youth
that dislodged the poisoned morsel,
and when I would have left her to my men
suddenly she was all weepy talk...such a story!

When I found she was pedigreed
I thought, might as well keep her as not.

No question of bride-price, of course,
not with her father unsure of her worth
and his own family circumstance in disarray.
He paid handsomely to dispose of the issue.

She's been a good wife these thirty years,
well-behaved and a fine mother
and doesn't she still turn heads?
Yes, I've seen you looking. No fear.

I'll tell you a little secret, boys . . .
most nights before I visit her chambers,
I send up a draft of laudanum,
and on my honor, it's nearly as good
as that first time.

THE WEDDING IN HELL
SONYA TAAFFE

with souls to Greer Gilman

And the bridegroom in his blackened coat, burnt dry as charcoal, bitter flinders and dust: his face a barbed moon, baited with a smile, his fingers jeweled with the salt of tears and seed. The lace at his wrists tattered to vellum rags, fingerprinted in rust; the white of his hair like flowers from bone, cracked for marrow, withered on the stalk, and nodding dryly in nowhere's breeze. Hoarse, and honey-tongued. The gravity of malice pulls his voice leisurely, slow and loving, loathing, a dead tongue's caress on flinch and bruise. Rain; rust. Ageless as a curse. On his skin, the smell of iron sears.

And his bride in her stony veil, her apron wrung with blood: her nails blue as drowned lips, her sea-worn eyes dried to dull avidity. High-shouldered, raked with years; black as a tarred slate, pale as a pecked skull, her hair hauled up in a clatter of souls. The mortal tongs, to handle carrion. To pinch and pluck, to pry and prick: fledged with greed, she does not disdain. The hunt's toying aftermath clouds her like a reek. Flesh cold as sea-slicked stone, even in her lord's wedded hand, and where he burrows she will bite. No breath mists the mirror in her palm.

And all the blood-smutched company, the jostling beaks

and talons, a crowd of shadows in the ruined hall. The stone sweats, ice-ridden, crystallized to monstrosity: hunger bred on hunger, the dainties of gutted dream. A cupboard of souls. Candied innocence, with the new blood showing at a thumb-nail's split. The anise cloy of desolation. The ravens' breasts leer like moons.

And how do you like your new-wedded bride? A kiss.
A clip. *Now you can lay me down and love me.*
There is no third in this marriage bed.
Crows eat thee. Cock and eyes.

UNDER THE INFLUENCE
ERZEBET YELLOWBOY

What is it to spin—
to hold a thread of your own making
between your fingertips?

What is it to measure—
to determine the length and line
of someone else's existence?

What is it to cut—
to end it all, to snap it off,
to say *this is enough*?

Three sisters know
as they wield these powers
that what they make,
they must also sever.

These are not threads.
They are our very lives and we
can only live with what we've got
or what we have been given.

We have no sureties, you and I,
down here in the muck.
There is only life and the living of it
until they say it's done.

These three, however;
they remain when we are gone.
Each does their part and then
hands it over to a sister.

Such trust is beyond human comprehension.

She who spins.
She who allots.
She who is inevitable.

We know that we are puppets
pulled along, string by string.
We tell ourselves our fate is all our own
when it is not.

These three—call them what you will—
in timeless hands hold us
and when they decide to make that cut
we must all submit.

She spins, she counts, she cuts,
as we run to the shop, or catch the bus.
We live, we breathe, we die.
We are the lucky ones.

When we are gone, still these three
will go on about their business.
They can do nothing but
spin and count and cut.

SAID THE TREE TO THE AXE(MAN)
NIN HARRIS

Perhaps the dreaming of twigs
incites strange intersections,
rain-dappled walkways for
atomic feet on solitary passages

Within the webwork of wood,
patterns point towards firmaments
like rough-hewn sundials of rock

Perhaps each cycle of experience
like mandalas encoded within trunk and bark
is etched upon the skin as well.

Perhaps the dreaming of hair, pigments,
melanin,
cuticles, pores open or close,
orifices moist or dry
incite strange diversions

Perhaps I am more than just a color,
a percentage of melanin;
perhaps I am more than
inherited rituals—

an anthropological phenomena
or a chapter in
your cultural studies textbook

Perhaps I am every scar
every stretchmark
every bruise &
every laugh-line present—
within the weavework of
tissue, muscle and bones
patterns pointificate
towards hidden ontologies
that can never be encountered.

*

What, must I engage
with you in

"discourse"?

Such a laden word, fraught
like trees overburdened
with fruit refusing to drop &
waiting to rot on the branch.

I am no fragile and slender sapling
planted in temperate climes;
humidity does not inspire fear—
the buzz of tropical insects do
not provoke palpitations

I am a raintree
with gash-marks where some
axe has tried to conquer me—

the blade has broken against
the hardness of my bark, turned
rusty against softness where I host
and nurture myriad epiphytes.

I wear this blade,
appropriated, reclaimed
as a badge of strength

My roots dive and tease bedrock
tendrils of it will get drunk
on the evanescence of
a subterranean stream

My leaves are ever green
and know no seasons
regardless of minutes, seconds
I will feed off blood and excrement,
find nurture deep within
pungent, fertilized soil

Do you believe you are the first
to try to cut me down?

Do you believe you will be the last?

What, must I give of my words to you?
Careful, I'll extract far more
than you are willing to pay.

BIOGRAPHIES

Erik Amundsen has published a handful of stories and poems in places such as *Weird Tales* and *Mythic Delirium*. He lives behind a cemetery in central Connecticut. So far, his neighbors have been very quiet.

Elise Matthesen lives in Minnesota, surrounded by beads, metal, words, music, and people she loves. She has a jewelry business, a hearing impairment, fibromyalgia, arthritis, attitude, ingenuity, numerous publication credits, and many pairs of pliers.

Alison Campbell-Wise was born and raised in Montreal, Canada and currently lives outside of Philadelphia. Wise's work has appeared in *Story House, Insidious Reflections, Flesh and Blood*, and the anthologies *Time for Bedlam* and *Shadow Regions*.

Jessica Paige Wick lives near Los Angeles. In spite of wildfires, earthquakes, and the evil plottings of her nefarious cats, she often manages to produce fiction and poetry. Her work has appeared in *Star*Line, Chiaroscuro, Aoife's Kiss, Mythic Delirium* and *Ideomancer,* and is forthcoming in *Cabinet des Fees 2*. She also co-edits *Goblin Fruit* with Amal El-Mohtar.

Born in the Pacific Northwest in 1979, **Catherynne M. Valente** is the author of the *Orphan's Tales* series, as well as *The Labyrinth, Yume no Hon: The Book of Dreams, The Grass-Cutting Sword,* and four books of poetry, *Music of a Proto-Suicide, Apocrypha, The Descent of Inanna*, and *Oracles.* She has been nominated for the Rhysling and Spectrum Awards as well as the Pushcart Prize. She currently lives in Ohio with her two dogs.

Jennifer Rachel Baumer lives in Reno, Nevada, with her husband/best friend/sometime editor Rick and a rapidly expanding number of cats. When not writing fiction Jennifer can be found procrastinating on writing nonfiction, from which she makes a tentative living.

Mike Allen lives in Roanoke, VA with his wife Anita, a comical dog and a demonic cat. *The Philadelphia Inquirer* called his most recent collection, *Strange Wisdoms of the Dead*, "poetry for goths of all ages." Mike is a three-time winner of the Rhysling Award for speculative poetry, and his short stories have turned up recently in *Cabinet des Fées, H.P. Lovecraft's Magazine of Horror* and *Helix: Speculative Fiction Quarterly.* He's also editor of the poetry journal *Mythic Delirium* and the upcoming fiction anthology *Clockwork Phoenix.* By day, he's a newspaper reporter. Among his favorite assignments: a lengthy profile of the late great pulp writer Nelson Bond and two interviews with the inventor of The World's Only Ass-Kicking Machine.

JoSelle Vanderhooft's poetry has appeared or is forthcoming in a number of publications including *Dreams and Night-*

mares, Mythic Delirium, Goblin Fruit, Cabinet des Fees, Star*Line and several others. Her first full-length poetry collection *Ossuary* was just released from Sam's Dot Publishing. She is also the author of the novella *The Tale of the Miller's Daughter*, and has several books scheduled for release in 2008. Visit her at joselle-vanderhooft.com or at upstart-crow.livejournal.com

Lynne Jamneck is a South African expat living in Wellington, New Zealand. She's still getting used to the cold. Her fiction and nonfiction has appeared in *So Fey: Queer Fairy Fiction, Sex in the System: Stories of Erotic Futures, Technological Stimulation, and the Sensual Life of Machines, Distant Horizons,* and *Strange Horizons.*

Jeannelle Ferreira lives outside Washington, D.C. with her wife, her dwarf hamster, and a selection of cats ranging from megalomaniacal to Mahayana. She is finishing her second novel for Prime Books.

Karina Sumner-Smith is a twenty-something recluse, short fiction author and novelist-in-the-making. Writing seriously since her late teens, Karina's publication credits include stories in anthologies *Mythspring* and *Children of Magic,* as well as work placed in magazines such as *Strange Horizons, Lady Churchill's Rosebud Wristlet* and *Flytrap.* In addition to her writing and a new job with an IT consulting firm, Karina recently launched a jewelry design company with a friend, and so finds herself with massed quantities of beads and wire, and very little free time. She lives in Toronto.

Maura McHugh lives in the West of Ireland, where the mythic resonances of the countryside remain strong despite the influx of housing estates and mega shopping complexes. Her short stories have been published in *Cabinet des Fées* and the anthology *Fantasy*. Her web site is splinister.com

John Benson's poems have appeared in *Tales of the Talisman, Tales of the Unanticipated, Talebones*, and *Bare Bone*. He is editor of *Not One of Us* magazine and *The Best of Not One of Us*. John lives in Massachusetts and is a survey research director at a school of public health.

Sonya Taaffe has a confirmed addiction to myth, folklore, and dead languages. Poems and short stories of hers have been shortlisted for the SLF Fountain Award, honorably mentioned in *The Year's Best Fantasy and Horror*, and reprinted in *The Alchemy of Stars: Rhysling Award Winners Showcase, The Best of Not One of Us, Fantasy: The Best of the Year 2006*, and *Best New Fantasy*. A respectable amount of her work can be found in *Postcards from the Province of Hyphens* and *Singing Innocence and Experience*. She is currently pursuing a Ph.D. in Classics at Yale University. Her livejournal is Myth Happens, sovay.livejournal.com

Catherine L. Hellisen lives in South Africa and she likes her music loud and her stories dark and fragile. She studied graphic design before she realised how much she hated it, and took to writing instead. In her spare time she belly dances, spins poi, and watches far too much British comedy.

Sara Amis lives in Athens, Georgia, where she is attending the MFA program in Creative Writing at the University of Georgia. Former occupations include anthropology research assistant, fortune teller, actor/model, editor of a small SF 'zine, and, most disreputably, secretary. She writes poetry, fiction, and unidentifiable hybrids with blithe disregard for genre, and reads fairy tales whenever she can get them.

Shy and nocturnal, **Jennifer Crow** has never been photographed in the wild. She lives in a little house made of books, and recites poetry on her porch when the moon is full. If you want to catch up with her work, you can find it in recent issues of *Illumen*, *Star*Line*, and *Mythic Delirium*, as well as online at *Strange Horizons* and *Abyss & Apex*.

E. Catherine Tobler climbed mountains in her youth, in a bright yellow coat, with shoes that were red, yellow, and blue, and made her feel like a clown. She endured. Writing, she decided, is not that much different. For more on her and her work, see her website at www.ecatherine.com

Shirl Sazynski believes in the pursuit of knowledge and all things beautiful—and an insoucient perception of gender, exploring the history of the beautiful male embraced in Japanese pop culture (www.bishoneninfo.com). A student at Hollins University, she is a regular contributor to *Animerica* magazine, editorial assistant at *Mythic Delirium*—and simultaneously attempting to learn ancient Greek, martial arts and how to play the harp—though not necessarily at the same time.

Mia Nutick lives in Portland, Oregon with a computer geek and far too many pets. She is a former managing editor and reviewer for *Green Man Review* and her work has appeared in *The Eloquent Umbrella, Cabinet des Fees, EOTU,* and *Mytholog.* "Braggadocio" is from her Wicked Fairy Apologist series, in which she explores fairy tales from different and sometimes surprising perspectives. She is currently working on the first novel in the WFA series.

Erzebet YellowBoy is co-editor of *Cabinet des Fees,* a journal of fairy tale fiction, and the founder of Papaveria Press, a private press specializing in handbound limited editions of mythic poetry and prose. Her stories have appeared in *Fantasy Magazine, Jabberwocky, Goblin Frui*t and *Mythic Delirium* and her novel, *Sleeping Helena,* is due out next year.

Nin Harris is a multi-medium and multi-genre storyteller (incorporating music, fiction, poetry and the visual arts). She has been an absconding law intern, an editor for educational books, a freelance theatre and book critic as well as a university instructor/lecturer. She is currently a Ph.d. student at the University of Queensland, Australia. More examples of her storytelling may be found at www.mythopoetica.com

"I tell you there is a wind that blows . . . . And I hear in the air something that is like the beating of wings, like the beating of vast wings. Do you not hear it?"—*Salome*